Eyes Wide Open

Poetry Inspired by Amsterdam

Melanie P. Falina

For Mike

Stay

Early morning
And coffee in hand
In a garden
On a canal
And my world is
Blissfully
Upside down

Every eye
Of the Dutch canal homes
Has opened
As light sparkles
In and out
Upon this burly
Salt and fresh water
Way

Expansive whirling arms
Spread wide in welcome
Pouring freshly
Brewed beer
And murmuring
Into my ear
"Stay"

Aeme-Stelle

First flush of dawn
Drinking
From the canal –
Stone beneath
My feet
But water
And water
And water
Everywhere that I
Can see –
I watch ripples
Etched by
Rembrandt
And feel that
Dewy
Chill in the air
Even on warmer days –
As the river
Flows from
South Holland
To where I stand
And around
And through me

About A Girl

Feet dangling over
Glass
Reflecting back
The hooks
And neck gables
Of tapering
Canal homes
We're here about
A girl

Boats loaded
With beer
And good cheer
Ask us to
Join them
And how fun
That would be
But we're here about
A girl

Bright evening
Easily mistaken
For glossy post-meridian
We take to
Winding steps
And landings
Space and breath
Both weighty
And clogged
But we're here about
A girl

And the room
She shared
Laughed with
Cried with
Her sister –
Newspaper photos
Of celebrities
And fashion
Upon the walls
Just like any other –
- every-
Other teenaged girl
Pulled at
My insides - - -

Trapped
And hiding
And then died
Anyway
And the air brimming
Within
These walls
Still thick with
Tribulation
Here she is still
Beautiful
And terrible
What's left here
About a girl

And I Walk

This town is
A body –
Breathing –
Feeling –
Abundant fluid
Pulsating through its veins –
I walk
And I walk
On so many paths
Beside and over
Water
Relenting to the trams
When finally tired
Riding these arteries
From one end
To the other
And back again
To more water
Late – and yet
The sun still
Hasn't gone down

Below Sea Level

Oh
Lady Amsterdam
Your high-standing
Poise –
Both bricks
And dusk kissed cheeks alike
Blush –
Coquettish
And yet
Unpresuming

Unblinking
I watch
The sun
Stash itself
Beyond
A row of
Slender homes –
And somewhere
Within at least
One of those vast
Windows
Oils are
Melding into water
And timelessly
Ever
Remaining below
Sea level

Bewitchment

As light begins
To slip from
The sky
A flow emerges
From
What seems
But a few
Lit windows
Yet caresses
Every –
Thing –
Cajoling
A glint of
Bewitchment
Upon
All the eye
Can see –
From the black
Iron rails
Lining bridges –
Spanning canals –
To the austere focus
Of bicycle spokes
Many as
The night's stars –
And a sampling
Of wrinkles and
Wavelets - - -
For the water
Always murmurs
At all hours

But particularly at night
In the
Venice of the North
And the
Smolder
Of café windows
Is more than
Willing
To give those
Words light

Ascent

Cast the eyes
Downward
Upon
Narrow stairways –
The slender
Treads
And seemingly
Tricky
Risers
Are mischievous –
Perilous
To a poor
Stranger's feet –
Wait
For the top
Wait
For the unwavering
Landing
To look out
Upon this sun-kissed
Town
Rising from the
Grachten
And soaring into
The sky
With so much glass
To reflect –
To showcase –
Open this city up
And present it to all

Discernment

Never have I seen
Flowers
Such as these –

The orange
Beneath the sun –

The blue
Bursting from a modest vase –

Rich pristine simplicity

Did they offer you
Comfort
Or ire
In those last two years?

Had you'd known
How much this would all matter
They'd say you
Were crazy
But what do they know

For maybe
We all need
To see the world
Through the eyes
Of the penniless
And through the discernment
Of the mad

Silky Ribbon and Conviction

Skies wide –
And higher
Than our eyes
Can see –
Down to the
Mirrored influx
Below –
Harness myself
With silky ribbon
And conviction
In glossy pointe shoes
To stand high and still
And regal
As the homes lining
This canal –
Then dancing
Atop one
Houseboat
To the next –
To the next –
Twirling
Upon another
Houseboat
To the next –
To the next –
Offering of myself
To the overflow
And polychrome
Of the setting
Netherlands' sun

Dusk on the Canal

Stillness
In a city that's ever moving
As the last
Rays of day
Inflame
The windows –
Enkindle the
Bow and berth –
Fragments from more than
Four thousand
Miles away
Tug tenderly at my
Pantleg –
And with a cross of
My legs
I kick them
Aside
And sip
Dutch beer
From a wet
Freshly washed
Glass

Day and Dim

We are serpents
Transplanted
Gliding through canal waters
Just beside
Dust displaced
By the bypast
Steps of Rembrandt
We incline to
The last glowing golds
Of day
Romping despite the shadows
Abaft the Night Watch
Sans the puff and feather
And fuss
We dawdle
About the day
And dim
Knowing not
Of a far off
Recrudescence
To this point on the globe
Measured
Sifting through sediment
Blithely
And all forged
And perched
And sun kissed
Atop

Of Course

Of course
There is a vase
Of tulips
– sitting delicately –
– placed properly –
In a large
Gaping window

Of course
The flush of petals
Gleamed
Versus
The chocolate binding
Of bricks

Of course
The flowers
Despite their innocence
Set in motion a titter
Or two
From tourists
Gliding by
And pushing on

But of course
The cognizance
Of tulip petals
Being silky and creamy and ever so pink
In that vase
Within that peering piece of glass
Is perfect

Even in Amsterdam
Especially in Amsterdam

And of course
One can't help
But smile

Solitary

Blossom petals
Amassing
Atop the glass-like stillness
Collected
In a lone skiff
And forgotten in pursuit of
Beguiling deeds

A sole duck
Sliding yet barely gliding
In the boat
Amid abandoned hush
Placidly
Content in the tight confines
Unruffled
And seemingly incurious
By the vastness
Of the rest of the canal

The Way

Set in place
For centuries
Yet ever in motion
Your limbs
Extended
Embracing
The rhythm –
The intent –
Of even the faintest breeze
And ever the howling gust
Swivels and swerves
Births it anew
Unto vigor
And exigency
And the surrounding expanse
Burgeons in
Silky turbans
Of yellow
Of white
Of red
En masse
Teetering
Side to side
Some moments
Or not the next
All one sees
Steered by the wind

Adagio

Though the tick
Is only heard down
At the roots
Of swelling tulips
There's a sovereign
Metronome
Tethered to all things
Within this canalside town

From the tempo
Of water's ripples
To the pulse
Of prismatic and silken swaying petals
Up to the ever shifting
Endlessly wakeful
Nomadic sky
And out from the swirling
Revolutions of windmill blades
Bound by the breeze
Methodical without motive

Carriageway

On my way to see Van Gogh
Smiling to myself
I muse
Beckett's *Waiting for Godot*
Knowing
One has nothing
To do with the other
But I am ever amused by
Plays on words
Rijksmuseum's underpass beckons
A shaded pardon
From the lucent verve
Of afternoon light
While my eyes
Forcefully focus
Bypast moments
Flicker peripherally
With the raucous
Of the carriageway
Now governed by
Aluminum and thin tires
Street musicians
Play to the pedestrians
On either side
A bountiful baroque piece
That I do not recognize
Far grandeur on the concrete
Than what I've paid
Handsomely for in the States
And it echoes
Flawlessly

Adding a haunting fragment
Of swell
And accession
But knowing better
Than to trip over
Any notes
Already released

Linkage

The first Dutch tulip
To set eyes
(and lips) upon
Was that of a beer glass
Sans notes of perfume
Within a warm spring breeze
But instead (slightly)
(Delightfully) bitter hops
In clinging lace
Which couldn't have been
More pleasing to me

The blushing hues of silk
Came later
Spines elongated
Wavering to a melody
Felt but not heard or seen

And not having expected
Otherwise
But even so
Still surprised
At the array
Of varied flowers
Everywhere
Kindred to the tulips
And yet solely dignified

Roots woven through the soil
Dipping further
To taste cool water

And tendrilled
Up to canal house hooks
Wrapped tight and
Gazing down
Upon the channel

Paint Maker

So many faces
Some well fed and
Outwardly genial
Some tired and
Some bothered to still be bothered
Or maybe I'm projecting
So many faces
Eyes locked onto the man
Whose eyes
Swam in each of their seas
In a room
Perhaps too dim
To see what is
As it truly is
Yet the glow
Spills forth
From every one
But maybe I'm projecting
As he simply did
With his Earth pigments
Presumedly too little
While painting so many

Convergence

Try to find
Stillness
In a city
That's ever in motion
For even the Bloemenmarkt
Bursting with its bounty
Of flower petals and souvenirs
Bobs and sways
Wafts and sways –

Despite all the bad
The sour
In the world
We've become more connected –
When moats
Evolve to passageways
There are more bridges
And fewer walls
And ever evident
To the beauty
And tragedy
That we belong
To one another

Time Capsule

We held hands
In the night
Beneath the soft
Yet profuse light
Of a fulsome lamppost
That was also guarding a bike
– there is always a bike –

And the shadows
Moved like cats
While a tranquil and stumpy cat
Sat
Still as a shadow
In a lofty window
Backdropped by books
And stacks and stacks
Of them

Grachten

There seems
To always be

Jewels

Bobbing

In the canals

Diamonds
In the a.m.

Rubies and sapphires
At night

Twinkling

Like stars

And sometimes

Venus or Mars

Up in the sky

Polarity

As I look out
Across the water
At least one hundred eyes
Are wide and bright
And unblinkingly
Looking back at me
And yet
There's a stillness
A serenity
In the night air here
A drop of noiselessness
Of placidity
Amid the bustling babel
A breath
Taken in
Then let out
Leadenly
In the center
Of a windstorm

Dutch Shadows

Only in this city
Does sunlight
Appear to skirt
Down curving streets
And along the steep
Cobblestone footways
The way fog
Rolls into other towns
Seemingly sideways
Instead of from above
Making us all
Tall in shadows
Regardless of our height

A World in Bloom

Young ladies
Dressed as flowers

Bowls for breakfast too
Filled with flowers

For never have I
Not appreciated
The delicate
Silken sight or
Aroma of Earth

But now
In my life
For some reason
It matters so much more

Bike baskets
Brimming over
With flowers lining
Bridges crowning the canals
And I'm happy
To have come
To Amsterdam

Your Waters

Both days and nights
Drinking beers
In windmills

And a little dog
Named Toby
Who liked us instantly
For our lunch

Combined hours
Roaming
As I have everywhere
I've been in Europe
But the walks
Are like people
And I have
Shaken your hand
Sweet Amsterdam
Looking into your big eyes
And haphazardly
Navigating the veins of bike paths
Trying desperately
To stay out of wheeler's ways

Both morning and evening
In the sun

And your waters
Dear Amsterdam

And a small seashell

Found on the banks
Of a canal
Now has a new home
Across the Atlantic

Also by the author:

❖ *Gaslit Shadows: Poetry Inspired by New Orleans* ©2014

❖ *French Quarter Rain: Poetry Inspired by New Orleans* ©2014

❖ *Crescent City Fog: Poetry Inspired by New Orleans* ©2014

❖ *Vieux Carré Days: Poetry Inspired by New Orleans* ©2014

❖ *Dark Days, White City: Poetry Inspired by Chicago in the Wintertime* ©2015

❖ *Whispers in The Courtyard*
(Poetry Inspired by New Orleans anthology including *Gaslit Shadows, French Quarter Rain, Crescent City Fog,* and *Vieux Carré Days*) ©2015

❖ *Spirits of the Old Square: The Things That Go Bump in a French Quarter Night* ©2015

❖ *River Baptized Beads: Poetry Inspired by New Orleans* ©2018

❖ *Rooftop Rhapsody: Poetry Inspired by Paris* ©2018

❖ *Spirits of the Prairie: The Things That Go Bump in a Windy City Night* ©2018

❖ *Dusk and Conjure: Poetry Inspired by New Orleans* ©2019

❖ *Roaming the Square Mile: Poetry Inspired by London* ©2019

❖ *Seeing The Other Side: Poetry Inspired by Cairo* ©2019

…and…

❖ *Cobblestone and Shadows: Poetry Inspired by Istanbul* ©2019

Melanie P. Falina on the Web...

Amazon:

www.amazon.com/author/melaniepfalina

Facebook:

www.facebook.com/PoetryByMelaniePFalina/

Goodreads:

www.goodreads.com/MelaniePFalina

Instagram:

www.instagram.com/poetry.by.melanie/

And the Official Blog:

https://poetryandplayinginthemud.blogspot.com/

Coming soon...

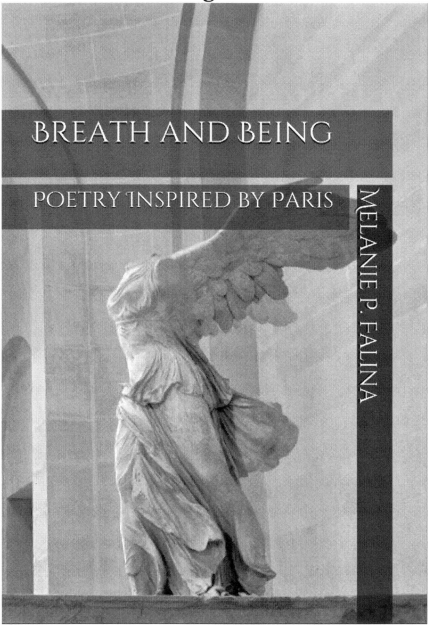

BREATH AND BEING

POETRY INSPIRED BY PARIS

MELANIE P. FALINA

The second installment in the
Poetry Inspired by Paris book series

Made in the USA
Columbia, SC
11 September 2019